Beauty Secrets

Redefining beauty through
inner healing, self-discovery, and self-development

By Stephanie Renee Parks

SJ Writing Services, LLC
Publishing
Columbia, South Carolina
https://sjwritingservice9.wixsite.com/website

Copyright © 2025 by Stephanie Renee Parks

First Edition: 2025

Book Cover Design
J-Shots Photography & Media/Clinton.jones127@gmail.com

Editing
SJ Writing Services, LLC.

ISBN: 978-1-967699-03-2

Table of Contents

Acknowledgement……………………….....................………….1

Introduction Beauty Is……………………………....…….......3

Chapter One: Confidence Is Key…....…………….……….…..6

Chapter Two: Loving the Skin You Are In ....…..17

Chapter Three: Finding the Beauty In Chaos………………..25

Chapter Four: Walking in Grace.. 35

Chapter Five: Trust The Process 49

Chapter Six: Live On Purpose 58

Chapter Seven: Change Your Hair, Start Over 68

Chapter Eight: Embrace Your Flaws……………...………….78

Chapter Nine: Glow Get It…....…………………..……….…86

Chapter Ten: Honor The Beauty That Is Deep Inside of You…....98

About the Author……………………….......................………107

-

Acknowledgment

First, I would like to give honor to my heavenly Father for creating me in his image and for preserving me when the enemy came to steal my innocence, kill my hope, and destroy my future; I thank my Lord for anointing me to carry out his purpose to spread love, and beauty to the world and the souls that are drawn to the light he gave me. I am thankful that because of his covering, I survived many battles and overcame many obstacles just to be able to use my gift of writing to lead some other young woman into their freedom and healing.

Secondly, I would like to give honor to my mother, Tonia Renee Williams-Medlock, who is now resting in the hands of the Lord, for deciding to give me life even when the odds were against her. Thank you, Mom, for raising me up in love and strength and for modeling the true essence of resilience before me. If it were not for your love and direction, I would not be the woman, mother, prayer warrior, and entrepreneur I am today. My mother was my best friend, confidant, and my support system, and I thank her for naming me Stephanie which means "crown," and for reminding me to never let life circumstances keep me from wearing mine well. I love you, momma.

I would also like to thank every mentor and role model whom I like to call my spiritual mothers For seeing in me the potential that I, at times, could not see in myself and for always encouraging me and helping me through the tough times. You ladies were evidence that God not only saw me but that he had a plan for my life, so I needed not to give up.

Lastly, I would like to honor the woman I am becoming. I am proud of you for trusting God through the hard times, for not letting the teenage pregnancy deter you from your dreams, for not letting the depression keep you down, for not letting the anxiety overtake you, for not allowing the suicide ideation and attempt win over your will to survive and live for your children, for not letting the abusive relationships taint your joy, for not letting the divorce steal your hope of loving again, for not letting death of your loved ones be the end of your faith walk and for simply never giving up! I honor your resilience, your strength, your determination, your kind heart, your boldness, your courage, your beauty, your classiness, your fierceness, your positivity, and your Godliness. Woman, you shine brightest, being exactly who God has created you to be in all your many facets, and I am excited to walk out this journey with you as God blows your mind as he elevates you with peace, joy, love, and prosperity all the rest of your life, I speak nothing but overflow over your entire bloodline from your children to your children's children and their children's children and may the healing and breakthrough you've received be used to break yokes of bondage off of every soul you encounter, blessings my beloved!

Introduction

Beauty is defined by a combination of qualities that pleases the aesthetic senses, especially sight. It is the state of being authentic and sincere in such a way that it extends love to first yourself, then to others. It feels real, safe, alive, playful, flowing, authentic, and life-giving. Beauty can be displayed with our fashion, hair, bodies, and faces but true beauty is displayed from the inside through our behavior and our attitude. Your Beauty is just an outward expression of the innermost parts of who you are.

Beauty is in who you are. Think about that. Who are you? When you can answer that question clearly and boldly, that is where beauty lies. It is your acceptance of yourself, not just what others see when they look at you. If no one ever called you beautiful, could you believe that you are, in fact, a creation of beauty? As you read this book, I pray that you, too, can discover that the true Beauty within you runs deeper than you even realized.

I know it sounds kind of cliché to refer to beauty in such an obsolete way because not many of us are looking inwardly to feel beautiful but instead are making sure that we can be affirmed by people for our physical attributes, but maybe it is time to consider that the reason why there are so many people committing suicide, or losing their joy to depression and even giving up on their dreams and aspirations is because they have lost their self-confidence. Some may even feel unworthy due to the lack of this very belief that they are not beautiful enough or special enough.

As you delve deeper into this book, my hope is that you too, will discover the missing pieces within your hearts and, embrace how beautiful you are, and even take notice of some unique ways that you are, in fact a work of beauty created by God.

This is not just a book that talks about superficial features and calling it beauty but it is an attempt to get you to see that in a world full of baddies, or the so-called real ones that you were born for a unique purpose and that stepping away from the trends and the norm of today would serve you with a new outlook on self-confidence, admiration for your authentic self, as well as, aid you in your pursuit of finding out who you are destined to become.

Listen Queen, as you read this book, I pray that you not only realize that you are beautifully and wonderfully made, that you realize that your crown is in your soul and not just on your head, but also, to know that your beauty is where you discover your worth. My wish is that you begin to see where your true beauty lies and that when you begin to own it, and that is when you will truly be able to embrace being your own kind of beauty.

In the beginning God created the heavens and the earth; the earth was formless and empty, the bible says in genesis one that there was nothing but God's spirit hovering over the surface of the waters, then God spoke and said, "let there be light." I want to begin with the truth of the creation of beauty because I believe that once we understand that beauty itself is a gift from God, then we will understand how to define it in pureness and wholeness and not in the way that society has perverted the idea of beauty. After creating life

4

in many forms, the Lord spoke and said, lets us make human beings in our image then God blessed them and told them to be fruitful and multiply and fill the earth and subdue it, and after he saw all that he had created he said it was very good. You are Gods good thing that he created to bring beauty to the earth through your unique creativity, dominion, and the gift of love. In fact, you are an expression of Gods true love and his very idea of beauty.

John 8:25 "Who are you"? They Demanded. Jesus replied, "the one I have always claimed to be."

Matthew 6:34
"So do not worry about tomorrow, for tomorrow will bring its own worries. Today's trouble is enough for today.

Chapter 1

Confidence Is Key

It's so amazing how beauty changes lives. A style or even a little makeup, well nowadays, a full-face beat, can make a person feel their absolute best in just about an hour or two. An outfit that hugs the body just right and a pair of heels can give a woman the confidence that she needs to conquer all she aspires to conquer. Well, those things are just a small portion of what beauty really is. We often think the picture that gets the most likes on social media is what makes us the most beautiful, but true beauty is so much more than that.

Imagine being the most beautiful woman in the room with all the enhancements we add on to our image and still feeling insecure about your flaws or lack of perfection. Think about it.

Why do you think we sometimes measure our beauty based on what is on the outside, instead of what is on the inside? Now, Imagine being stripped naked in a room full of mirrors with no makeup on, and your hair in its natural state. How would you feel about yourself? If your answer is "not good," then it is time to take a deeper look at yourself; if your answer is "not sure," then take some time to rediscover yourself. Lastly, if your answer is good,

then think about what makes you feel so beautiful. Use that as fuel to live out your unique purpose on this earth.

Having strong self-esteem and confidence is beauty. You may ask, "Where does confidence come from?" Confidence is often defined as the feeling of trust and self-assurance arising from one's appreciation of their own abilities or qualities. Sometimes in life when we compare ourselves to others, it is not necessarily about what they look like but the traits and qualities that they possess. When you realize that each of us has our own uniqueness, you will learn the importance of not desiring to be someone else. Some of us fail to realize who we are and what we have to offer to the world. As children, some of us were not shown affection from our loved ones, or we were not affirmed as children by our parents. Some of us were raised to compete with other little girls in pageants or constantly compared to others. This could have had a direct effect on your self-esteem earlier on, planting seeds of insecurities in some aspect that were watered over time. So, the lack of confidence, at times, may be the presence of those little insecurities that took root in your mind and heart. Maybe the truth is that sometimes it is fear, such as the fear of not fitting in or being accepted for who you are. Whatever it is, we must choose to challenge every negative thought about ourselves and replace them with affirmations. Our affirmations should reinforce who we are and, better yet, who we are destined to become.

We were all created as an expression of God, each for a unique purpose. For that reason, it is important to walk in the light and image of who you were created to be. Being willing to let go of the things that no longer serve you will give you the ability to surrender to the version of you that looks like the power that was placed inside of you by the Creator. Therefore, it is time to break off anything that keeps you bound to that lesser version of yourself.

We have all had moments in our lives when we have encountered relationships, environments, and situations that made us pose the question, "AM I GOOD ENOUGH?" Maybe the relationship ended, you were rejected from a job opportunity, or you did not fit in within your community. Maybe you had a feeling of being the underdog or being unqualified. Whatever the situation was, did it rob you of the sense of confidence that you had? If we are honest, we all have questioned if we were good enough at times. As human beings, we display in our lives what was modeled in front of us as self-confidence. This sense of confidence may have been reinforced by family and friends, therefore creating inside of us a false sense of confidence that we are not actually sure of. We oftentimes make it the responsibility of others to affirm our worth instead of doing the inside work ourselves. Be bold enough to walk away from a version of yourself that pleases everyone else and allow God to renew you with a new confidence built on the foundation of who you were created to be.

What if we took the time to pray, fast, meditate, and seek GOD to ask about his thoughts regarding our lives and divine purpose on this earth? Could it be true that real confidence does not come from our thoughts about ourselves alone, but rather, what happens when we partner our thoughts with the thoughts of the Father in order to reclaim who we are in him? Once we choose to accept the invitation to walk out this newfound confidence from within that is fueled by joy, faith, hope, and the courage to be set apart from everyone else, that is when we will be able to see God's glory in our lives. It is important to see yourself in the image of the Creator because your perception of yourself affects your vision and your energy, so love yourself, walk confidently, share your unique talents, and let your good vibes flow.

Affirmation:
"I *am happy and content with myself, I am fearfully and wonderfully made. I am more than enough, I am beautiful in mind, body, and spirit!*"

Self-confidence is the key that unlocks every hidden potential that is within you. It leads you to fulfilling your destiny on this earth. Let us sit aside purpose and destiny for a second and digest the reason self-confidence is so important in life and how it affects you.

We live in a society where we are driven by the pleasures that this life can offer us, so why is it that only a fraction of the population is able to turn their dreams into goals and those goals into reality? The people who choose to go after their dreams, even when there is opposition present in their lives, are those who are confident enough to pursue their goals, even if they are scared. Your faith in your God-given abilities is what produces the confidence needed to achieve all that God has placed on your heart. This is the epitome of self-confidence and, a testament to how self-confidence and faith in God work together to produce exceptional results in your life.

Oprah Winfrey said, "The biggest adventure you can take is live the life of your dreams. Oprah faced many obstacles in her career, including dealing with people who were close to her saying that she would not amount to much in her career.-*quora.com*
 It was the confidence she had within herself and her ability to add something different to the television industry that allowed her to evolve in her career and in her life regarding her self-worth.

Self-confidence is best developed when spending quality time alone with God, takes priority over spending all of your time with people and in relationships; that does not serve whom God has created you to be! When you prioritize spending time with yourself, you choose to allow transformation to happen within yourself. This develops the character you will need to step into the next phase of your calling! Most of the time, we lack confidence because we tend to pay more attention to everyone else's greatness instead of creating space for our greatness to be unleashed. As you continue reading this book, I challenge you to take your POWER back. I challenge you to commit to setting aside time each day to pray, fast, meditate, spend quality time with the Lord, and rediscover yourself in an entirely new way!

"Your beauty should not come from outward adornment, such as elaborate hairstyles and the wearing of gold jewelry or fine clothes.

Rather, it should be that of your inner self, the unfading beauty of a gentle and quiet spirit, which is of great worth in God's sight."
1 Peter 3:3-4 (NIV)

Beauty is in the eye of the beholder.
Love yourself first and walk in confidence,
because confidence is beauty.

Journal your thoughts

Chapter 2

Loving the Skin You Are In

Beauty comes in all shapes, forms, colors, and creeds. It has no limits except the limitations that you have placed on yourself. Who does not want a nice round booty, small waist, perky breasts, and a pretty face? Many of us are trying to reach and keep this type of image. We sweat for hours in the gym, and we go on extreme diets, hoping that our curves fill out exactly right, to wear those round-bottom jeans and crop tops with our heels. Oh, and do not forget your 24-inch bundles that flow past your silhouette. Yes, that is beautiful. But what if you have all of that, all the attention that comes with it, and you still feel like you are not enough? Okay. Come on now. I am not the only one who has been acknowledged as the prettiest one in the room, yet felt the most insecure at times. I didn't feel this way because of my looks but because of my lack of being fully confident in my own gifts and talents. Thoughts of not being pretty enough or skinny enough have haunted many of us in certain seasons of our lives. When we see other women with what we believe is the perfect body, the perfect hair, or the perfect face, all we see is what we lack instead of what we are packing.

Every obstacle you have encountered, believe it or not, has shaped you into the person that you are now. The fact that you got through it gets you one step closer to revealing your true beauty.

Knowing who you are matters. It is the essence of who you are that is the most beautiful part of you. You must stop self-sabotaging by pointing out all your flaws and talking down to yourself. This behavior is usually a default setting that we have embraced subconsciously due to past trauma. Maybe you were teased as a child, grew up in an abusive home, or were not affirmed enough. Maybe you have been abandoned by people you love and trusted during a vulnerable time in your life, and you thought you could never recover from the trauma of not feeling that you were good enough. Whatever the situation was, know that it was never because you were not enough. Instead of self-deprecating behaviors, acknowledge that you are unique, and that there is no one else like you. God allowed each obstacle in your life to raise up certain characteristics within your heart that would soon reveal to you, your divine uniqueness and what your sole purpose is in the earth.

Instead of transforming your outer appearance, it is time to make a transformation inwardly. Yes, I am talking about a radical transformation that can only come from being at peace with yourself. The type of peace that allows you to value who you are and what you have instead of striving to live up to the expectations that society and culture place on you. Working on your inward beauty must first start with prayer.

Pray that God heals those broken places on the inside of you that hinder you from seeing the beauty on the outside. Pray for an inward transformation that allows you to see who you are as a person and what you bring to the world. It does not matter what other people think about you but what you think about yourself, Because when the relationships end and the crowd is gone, you will be left with yourself, and whatever your inner voice says you are. While showing up as your best self, it is important, to see what is inside of your heart that will help to propel you into your destiny.

Affirmation

"I am beautiful inside and out; I am unique, and there is no other person like me ".

Thank you for making me so wonderfully complex! Your workmanship is marvelous-how well I know it. *Psalm 139:14 NLT*

Beauty Secret #1

Beauty is in the eye of the beholder. Love yourself first and walk in confidence because confidence is beauty.

Beauty Secret #2

Accept yourself. Accept that there is no one else in this world like you, and that is what makes you who you are.

Beauty Secret #3

Take a moment to look at yourself in the mirror each day, point out something that you love about you. Own that thought and believe it!

Journal your thoughts

Write a letter to your
past self, offering kind
words of understanding
and empathy for the
struggles you have faced

Chapter 3

Finding the Beauty in Chaos

Have you ever taken the time to reflect on your life? The Early morning rush to work, or taking your kids off to school, finding time to cook a decent meal for your family or watching a movie with your children to spend some quality time with them? How about dealing with the issues that prevent those things from happening seamlessly every day? Take time daily to reflect on your life and find the beauty in the simple things. Otherwise, if you are not careful, everyday chaos can leave you feeling down on yourself and unable to move forward to your next blessing. Take inventory on all of the ways the Lord has made for you, and thank Him for even the toughest of times. In those times are strength and grace.

At times when things are happening around us that we cannot control, it can leave a lasting imprint of discouragement, desperation, and defeat on our hearts. This can cause us to seek comfort in people and things that only end up creating more damage to our souls. Discouragement, desperation, and defeat can even strip us of our confidence and contentment. We often doubt that we are worthy of happiness when we feel like we have failed to get life right. But rest assured, if you do not get overwhelmed but rather embrace all of life's obstacles, you will discover the lesson in it. God will reveal to you why certain things happened in your life and how those things were necessary for your growth.

Growth and developing spiritually, emotionally, and mentally are key components in discovering who you are and why you were placed on the earth. Often, chaos is not a sign that you are doing things wrong. It is often confirmation that all things are working together in your life to stir up in you the very thing that you will need in order to reach your highest potential and gain awareness of what you are supposed to be in life. Chaos in your life is a sign that the enemy has peeked into your future and seen all the victory that is connected to your life and maybe the beauty in a chaotic life is finding out what you are made of.

Strength, power, and wholeness can be found when you are faced with chaotic situations in life. Once you have learned from those difficult times, accepted the unpredictable, and come to the realization that God has a plan for your life. You will learn that even in discord, there is a strategy to catapult you into your destiny!

This is beauty when you think about it because it leaves room for you to gain wisdom about who you are in the kingdom and what your uniqueness is designed for. Sometimes, God must shake up your life to fix your life, and sometimes it is necessary to face adversity so that you may have a desire to seek the face of the Lord Jesus, for help and guidance. The Bible says in Psalm 46:1 that God is a present help in times of trouble. So, chaos is necessary so that we may be pruned and purged of all the traits that are not of the Father. We must ask ourselves the question "Who am I now?" and be still enough to hear what God says about us. A good father affirms his child just like our Father in heaven. Our Heavenly Father will affirm us, give us a new name, and identity that resonates in the likeness of who He is within us.

"Yesterday was a canceled check, tomorrow is a promissory note, and today is the only cash you have so spend it wisely"- Kay Lyons. The statement made by this romance author is quoted to put emphasis on how important it is to not waste time on the things that are out of your control but instead to make room for what is coming next in your life. Matthew 6:34 KJV says it best, *"So don't worry about tomorrow, for tomorrow will bring its own worries, today's trouble is enough for today."* God wants us to seek Him, and He will give us what we need to have for the next stage of our lives. Isn't it true that we can always find something wrong in our lives?

Why do you think that such thoughts creep into the mind to cripple us in some way, hindering our progress to greater? If the enemy can keep you repeating the cycle of negative self-talk, he knows that he can delay you from the promises that are attached to your life.

"There is death and life in the power of your tongue and the Bible says that those who love it will eat its fruit," so be mindful about the thoughts you think towards your life so that there are no open doors for satan to come in and confuse and derail you from your path.

Instead, realize that we do not have to do life alone. God is always with us, and He will even send us the people who are assigned to our next.

I have experienced so much chaos in my own life. When I look back, I am amazed that I made it through the darkest times of my life, feeling alone. But, I know that it was God that brought me through each time and better than I was before. Although I lost people I loved along the way, the right people came at the right time to lift me up and helped to either guide or push me to my next. Though it did not feel good at the time, I now see how those times grew me as a woman and as a believer and gave me the privilege of learning myself and God in a new way. I have learned so many valuable lessons that were needed to show me the areas within myself that would not serve where I was and am going. Most importantly, the lessons strengthened my awareness so that I would not look backwards.

I now shine from a different place inside of me because I am no longer weighed down by my troubles, hurts, and disappointments, but rather, I am a better, a more resilient me. I know that I can do all things through Christ which strengthens me and affirms who I am in Him; whole and perfectly imperfect! *"I find peace in knowing that even when I miss the mark or stumble and lose my way, God is still with me putting my life back on a path of wholeness and righteousness.*

But I now know that God is bigger, and I rest in the fact that, "This too shall pass." I am taking the steps God has ordered in my life to redefine who I am, and whose I am in the sight of God, and it gives me the freedom to embrace all that I am and not settle for a lesser version of me.

I challenge you to seek out the positive side of every unfavorable

28

circumstance in your life; find peace within your soul and watch how your spirit has elevated you to another level of being. I'm not saying be blind to the lessons that God may be allowing you to learn from the chaos, because a lot of things that occur in our lives have been a result of our own disobedience. We must take notice of how our choices have affected our lives, then make the necessary changes with the help of the Lord. What I am saying is to not see trouble and begin worrying, stressing, doubting, and just speaking negativity because that is a trap and a never-ending cycle.

Instead, relax, and know that if God allows it, He knows something that you don't. It is for a purpose that is unknown to you. Gods got you covered; He just wants our trust and that we fully surrender to HIM even in the face of chaos. When we look back after the smoke clears, and we are different, with new revelation of what we are made of, the beautiful thing is, we get to walk renewed and strengthened for the next battle.

Journal your thoughts

Reflect on your relationships and identify areas where you may need to set clearer boundaries. Write down situations where you struggle with setting boundaries and role-play how you might say "no" in those situations with respect and clarity.

Chapter 4

Walking in Grace

There are times in our lives when we are just doing our best. We often want to be acknowledged for our efforts, but most of the time we have not even taken the time to acknowledge them ourselves. As parents, spouses, significant others, and working citizens, whether you are a single parent or an entrepreneur, we all experience obstacles in our daily lives. With this being a fact for all humankind, we must take time each day to extend grace to first ourselves and then to others. I know it sounds easy, but sometimes we find it easier to affirm others in their well-doing than we do ourselves. It is spiritual suicide to take on so much daily and then choose not to release, unwind, and then show some gratitude towards yourself for just making it through the day in one piece.

Walking in grace is a conscious act of the heart; or rather, an invitation to release all the burdens that weigh us down each day. We are able to do this through prayer and meditating on the Word of God. Then, we can accept the gift of grace into our hearts that we do not deserve but which God freely extends to us. This practice also allows us to receive the gift of forgiveness and gratitude so we may then act and respond with love. This is heart work, and it not only makes you feel better, but this grace also invites positivity, love, and prosperity into your life.

In this chapter, I will share three practical ways you can be more mindful and intentional in walking in grace each day. Although there are more than three ways, these are three of my favorite practices that have really helped me to heal my brokenness and walk forward in my journey to wholeness. I pray it will give you some insight into your journey to wholeness, love, and peace.

1. *Start each day with Prayer, Positive Affirmations, and Meditation.*

What is the first thing you do every morning when you open your eyes? Do you investigate your phone to check your email, or social sites? Do you spend time laying idol thinking about all the tasks the day has set before you? If you know that these are some of the things you do when your eyes open to a new day, I challenge you to change your pattern and to spend some time praying and first thanking God for a brand-new day and all the new mercies that will follow.

Praying prayers like:
"Lord, thank you for this new day. I ask that you order my steps today and that you go before me in every room and set the atmosphere for positivity, victory and harmony, in Jesus Name, Amen." This is what I call, commanding your day and setting the tone in which God can work on your behalf to bring about peace and prosperity.

One thing that the Bible speaks of is intentionality. It reads in Psalm 37:23 NIV *"The Lord makes firm the steps of the one who delights in him";* the Word firm in the Hebrew, "firm" often translates to words like "steadfast," "unwavering," or "established," conveying the idea of being strong, fixed, or stable. Specifically, the Hebrew word "עָמַד" (amad) is frequently used to mean "stand firm,"

36

suggesting unwavering commitment and resolve, particularly in matters of faith and obedience. This word spoken by King David, describes the character of righteousness. Verse 24 of that same passage states, *"Though he may stumble, he will not fall, for the Lord upholds him with his right hand."*

Being intentional about your day helps us to prepare our hearts and minds for what God has ordered us to do on that day, knowing that he is the head of our destiny. The same passage in the KJV reads, *"The steps of a good man are ordered by the lord, and he delighted in his way."*

Prayer is a vital part of having a successful life as believers, because we understand that in order to walk in God's purpose for your life, we must first consult with Him, offering praise and gratefulness, making our request unto the Lord and asking for His Divine guidance to accomplish His will, because God knows the plans He already has for us as stated in Jeremiah 29:11. The Lord says in the book of Matthew 6:31-33 KJV, *"Therefore take no thought, saying, what shall we eat? Or, What shall we drink? Or, Where shall we be clothed? For after all these things do the Gentiles seek; for your Heavenly Father knoweth that ye have need of all these things. But seek ye first the kingdom of God, and his righteousness, and all these things shall be added unto you."*

When we pray, we are calling on heaven's resources to back us in our dealings and we are showing God that we trust in Him to direct us on a path that will accomplish His will and to provide us with all that we need. Prayer also allows us to have deeper intimacy with the Lord. It gives us the opportunity to be vulnerable with our Heavenly Father. God wants us to worship Him in spirit and in truth; so, when we pray we should talk to God as we would our parents, close friends, or therapist because it builds a greater line of communication where we can not only release but also receive from Him.

Positive Affirmations are so important because we are spiritual beings not just made from dirt but created by God's Word! We were made in God's image, Genesis 1:26 KJV, and God is the WORD. The book of John 1:1 KJV, states *"In the beginning was the Word, and the Word was with God, and the Word was God."* So, if we are made in the image of God and God was the Word and *"All things were made by him, and without him was not anything made that was made."* verse 3, then that means that Words are so important to our spirit man. We know that *"death and life are in the power of the tongue; And they that love it shall eat the fruit thereof, Proverbs 18:21 KJV.*

Therefore, positive affirmations can be an essential component for creating a fulfilling life of abundance, love and fruitfulness! This can include simply reciting God's promises over your life, or simply declaring what you want to see come to pass in your life. Speaking positively over yourself, despite life's challenges, gives us the hope and confidence to walk into our divine purpose equipped to conquer any task set before us. Verses like *"I am fearfully and wonderfully made", Psalm 139:14, or "I can do All things through Christ which strengtheneth me," Philippians 4:13,* helps us to command the day

38

and affirm our place in God, that no matter what comes our way, we shall overcome!

Other positive affirmations can simply affirm what you believe about yourself; for example, looking in the mirror daily and stating, "I am beautiful" or "I am wealthy," Can give you a sense of value and can attract self-assurance and value beyond money since beauty is an internal attribute that reflects outwardly while wealth is something that can include health, spiritual maturity, family, and possessions. Speak over yourself daily and watch how each word materializes into reality in your life. Beginning each day with positive affirmations is essential to armoring your mind and spirit to handle whatever the day brings, but it also allows you to create what you want to see that day!

Meditation is an essential part of commanding your day! Biblically, it involves slowly thinking or reciting scripture to focus attention until the words become part of who you are.

Psalm 1:2-3 NIV encourages us to, *"Delight in the law of the LORD, and who meditates on his law day and night. That person is like a tree planted by streams of water, which yields its fruits in season and whose leaf does not wither-whatever they do prospers."* This expresses how grounding ourselves in the Word of God through meditation helps us to succeed in all that we do daily. Psalm 119:15-16 says, *"I meditate on your precepts and consider your ways. I delight in your decrees; I will not neglect your word."* Joshua 1:8 instructs people to *"Meditate on the Book of the law day and night."* This instruction teaches us to study God's Word regularly in order to understand God's will for our lives. Even Jesus meditated on the Word of God which gave Him the ability to withstand being tempted by the devil in the wilderness without succumbing to sin. Meditation is not just about being still and quiet; rather, it is an opportunity to memorize the Word of God so that we may receive God's will, His way! When we meditate, however, as it relates to being still, we give God an open channel to speak back to us, direct us, and even give us divine insight that is not written in the Bible but is a special message to us from the Holy Spirit. The Bible states in Psalm 46:10 NIV, *"Be still, and know that I am GOD, I will be exalted in the earth."* Being still takes intentional focus, and it can be hard to meditate on God's Word without stillness therefore meditating the conventional way is also an asset to commanding your day, because it offers to you a time to slow down and indulge in some quiet time that allows the Holy Spirit to speak to us.

Praying, reciting positive affirmations over yourself, and taking the time to meditate are tools that can offer you support in your daily journey to discovering yourself through the eyes of God. I believe and have experienced the power of these acts and their ability to aid in building a stronger spiritual life, which leads to better decision-making and thriving life in Christ! I urge you to try them and watch God transform your life.

2. *Stop and Breathe.*

Did you know that when you are under pressure, your muscles tense up causing less oxygen flow to your brain. Due to the lack of

40

oxygen to your brain, you can lose access to cognitive function which causes you to lose focus. When life puts pressure on you, it is important to stop and breathe so that you can renew your strength, oxygenate your blood flow, and take time to take care of yourself while striving to get there! What good is getting there if you lose yourself in the process? There can be a position of success in your career, finally experiencing financial freedom, the accomplishment of a personal goal, or whatever you are striving for in your life. No matter what your (There) is, WALK LIGHT, remember that God already has a plan for your life, and you will arrive there in His divine timing.

Jeremiah 29:11 (NIV) reminds us of this when God speaks.

"For I know the plans I have for you," declares the LORD, *"plans to prosper you and not to harm you, plans to give you hope and a future."* When we surrender our lives to Christ, we exchange our plans for his perfect will and plan for our lives, and we must be willing to allow God to be God over our decisions and our paths, we must simply be Still. *In Psalm 45:10 He says, "Be still, and know that I am God." 2 Corinthians 12:9 says, "My grace is sufficient for you, for my power is made perfect in weakness."*

These declarations are why we should always walk in grace knowing that we will be victorious through any circumstances. So be kind to your mind, body, and spirit; all things are working out for your greater good.

3. *Sign off social media and be in the moment.*

   Social media can be a distraction. How often do we wake up and the first thing most of us do is grab our phones and log into social media to see what everyone else is doing? How many times have we been on vacation with family and been distracted by our phones? We may be trying to capture our highlight reels instead of taking time to just be present in that moment and allowing ourselves to bond with our loved ones. Understand that every moment in your life is a divine moment. No matter how small it may seem, each moment we experience in life teaches us something about who we are, what we have, and why we are here.

Divine alignment is about recognizing God in even the trivial things, so be sure to cherish every moment in your life.
Proverbs 16:9 says, "*In their heart's humans plan their course, but the LORD establishes their steps.*"
Enjoy the journey!

Taking time to pray, recite positive affirmations, meditate, as well as taking a moment for yourself to just breathe, and log off of social sites to be one with yourself, can help to align you with God's will for your journey. Grounding you in who you are, whose you are, and whom God has designed you to become! It is just a beautiful journey of becoming the best version of yourself, a version that God can use to fulfill His purpose through you on earth! Walking in Grace is no easy task, and it can be hard at times, but trust in the Lord and allow him to renew you in Him.

Note:

Each of our experiences prepares us for our destiny. Walking in grace means that we may not always get it right. No one is perfect, so it is important to shake off the weight of being all together and just embrace the learning process of life. When you get off course, do not condemn yourself or speak negatively about yourself because your words are powerful, rather, understand that you can get back on course. It is not the end. You will win!

Walking in grace gives us the ease to enjoy our lives. God does not want us to waste time worrying just to die and enter heaven. The purpose for his reduction of Himself to enter the earth was so heaven could be manifested here. He wants us to live life to the fullest and abundantly, so; relax and walk light, beautiful!

Journal your thoughts

Create a self-care check-
list for the week, listing
at least three activities
that make you feel
grounded and content.
How do these activities
help, to you?

Chapter 5

Trust The Process

Life is a continuous growth process. Setting goals, both short-term and long-term, can help you keep track of your progress. No matter what plans we make, though, it is important to trust in the process by which God chooses to conduct those plans through us. I like to say, "Leave some room for God to disrupt your plans for His own since He already knows what the expected end is supposed to look like." As you evolve, rest your thoughts and plans in the hand of our Lord and Savior, Christ, because He is in control. It is His will that will surely happen. The promises of Jeremiah 29:11 declare that God has a plan for us, and they are plans for good and not for evil to give us a future and hope. When we align our thoughts with those of the Father through spending time in prayer and meditation, it is inevitable that He will order our steps according to His will. The steps of the Lord will be clear, although you will not know his full plan, and most importantly, you will hear his voice directing you.

I don't know about you, but I would rather be in God's perfect will than in a whirlwind caused by my own will and desire. To be completely honest, this truth was revealed to me by living previously out of the will of God. I created a life that I thought would satisfy my brokenness and found myself in situations, and even relationships that were the polar opposite of what God wanted for my life. I was standing in God's way, yielding to my own understanding, and going with the motions because I was in His permissive will instead of His perfect will for my life. There were moments in my life when my way led me down a road of depression, anxiety, health issues, and emptiness while searching for love in all the wrong places. The Lord allowed all I have been through to strengthen me for where He has me now and for the plans He has for me, But honey, He allowed me to have it my way; He allowed the hurt, the doubt, the struggle, and the disappointments to occur until I decided that I was tired of living that way. It was not until I decided to invite the Lord into every area of my being and choose His way that He could fully direct me. You will receive so many signs that will show you whether or not you are off course. Pay attention to the areas of your life that do not bear fruit. It can be that the outcome of a situation is costing you the fruit of God's spirit, which is love, joy, peace, forbearance, kindness, goodness, faithfulness, gentleness, and self-control (Galatians 5:22 NIV). The Word tells us in *Matthew 7:18-20 that "A good tree cannot bear bad fruit, nor can a bad tree bear good fruit. Every tree that does not bear good fruit is cut down and thrown into the fire, therefore by their fruits, you will know them."* What God is saying to us is that if we examine our lives, we will know what things we must let go of and turn away from by the outcome it produces in our lives. In other words, our afflictions can be signs that we are off track and not operating in the will of God. But those things are only allowed, to further develop us in the areas that God wants to use us. The beauty of it is that we are being covered and directed by God to really discover who we are in Him and what our purpose is in the earth. Just like David, each stage of our journey is allowed to get us ready for that moment to take down the goliaths in our lives and even the goliaths from generations before us. This journey leads us to not only discover ourselves but God also revealed in a more profound way.

Beauty Secret

Meditate and pray for 15 minutes each day on God's promises for your life. Write down your current goals and desires and ask God what He wants to do in each area, then wait to hear his direction.

Be Specific!

Seek God's will in the process and allow Him to show you what moves to make. In Matthew 7:7 scripture tells us to *"Ask, and it will be given to you; seek, and you will find, knock, and it will be opened to you."* Although in this process, we can oftentimes feel lost or alone, making up our own way in the wilderness of life's transitions, we must rest in the fact that it's all working for us, as stated in Romans 8:28 "And we know that all things work together for good to those who love God, who are called according to his purpose." Because we were chosen, we all will face our share of persecution, pain, and struggle. That's why the Lord stated in Luke 3:23 NIV, "Whoever wants to be my disciple must deny themselves and take up their cross daily and follow me." Trusting in your process of personal growth and spiritual development encompasses the act of dying daily to your old ways of being and seeing your life so that you may be purified for the will of God. But it is just part of this process of becoming a better you through the love and sacrifice of our Lord and Savior Jesus. Endure this process and trust that you are being equipped for such a time as this!

Imagine your ideal self; how you look, feel, and act. Then identify one small action you can take today, that brings you closer to this vision.

Chapter 6

Live On Purpose

"Life is short." You hear most people say, but I disagree! Life is what you make it. We live with this concept of time that makes us rush through life, hoping to arrive there on time. And where is there? And whose time are we on? The only one who knows where we are to end up and at what appointed time is God. The time we race against is that in which the world says. You have heard it before: marry by the age of twenty-five, have children by age thirty, establish a successful career by the age of thirty-five, retire at the age of sixty-five, and so on. If we continue trying to live up to this status quo, we will never truly live up to our fullest potential. Life will happen, the car will break down, the bills will keep rolling in, and people will come and go, but God promises us to have life and have it more abundantly if we choose to live and rest in him; all these things will be added to us. Do not let life live you. Live life! You have the authority to command your day; you have the power to overcome every obstacle standing in your way. The Bible says that there is life and death in the power of the tongue, so your life will reflect what you say. Therefore, we must say what we want to see and not what we see! Sounds weird, right? Well, what if I told you that what you say is hindering your progress to purpose as well as what you think? It is biblical! Proverbs 18:21 says death and life are in the tongue, and those who love it will eat its fruit. When we live according to our divine purpose, we then understand that we inherit the same power that our Lord possesses, so when we speak with positivity, love, gratitude, and peace, our life will reflect those things because you will attract what you are.

My mother gained her heavenly wings not long ago, but I remember hearing her say she was sick and tired; when her patience ran out for whatever life was throwing her way, she would state, "I'm sick and tired, and I'm sick and tired of being sick and tired." Yes, she faced much sickness in her lifetime, and it was stage 4 lung cancer and her catching COVID-19 that caused her to pass away suddenly, but while she was undergoing treatment, I often encouraged her to speak more positively and against what she felt. So, when she was not feeling her best, she agreed that she would tell me that she was healed or that she was getting better; she continued this daily, and when I would try to cheer her up, I would ask, "How is my pretty lady today?" She would reply, I'm getting better, and it seemed to work because, according to her chemotherapist, her labs were looking better each week. Although she seemed very weak at times, I could tell that she was actually starting to feel better! Weeks went by, and the family started to roll in to offer their support to her, which allowed her to let her guard down and just be in the moment, but sadly, the very last thing she said to me was to take care of myself and my three boys, and when I asked her, "Well, you sound great, how is my pretty lady?" She replied, "I am sick, and I am tired!

As my heart began to fall into my stomach, I realized that if she was back at this negative self-talk, she was giving up. She passed away the very next day. My mother's life taught me so much about life; though she faced many obstacles, she remembered to smile, dance, and help those in need, and she did the things that made her happy, but most of all, her resilience was evidence of her trusting in the Lord even when life got tough. She simply LIVED!

Living on purpose takes courage, and to do so we must first realize that we have everything that we need to do so. Take a moment to just reflect on what brings you joy, what lifts your spirit, and what are the things that set your soul on fire. That is where your purpose lies. Shut out the many distractions, lean into yourself, and ask yourself, *who am I? What do I want out of life, and why?* Find your reason for being and never cease to strive to become that person you envision yourself becoming. There is so much more to who you are, and once you discover your passion, you will discover your purpose; then, you must decide to live each day from that place!

Each stage of life requires a different version of who we are, and we must be careful not to put limits on ourselves when we are called to much more in our life!

The very essence of who you are is evidence that you were created to add to the world something that is not already present. The way you see the world around you shapes you but be careful not to allow it to change your authenticity. One way that I have learned to truly live on purpose is to have just a few strong boundaries for yourself so that not just anyone can come into your life and impose their will, distracting you from what God has called you to. In some seasons of life, walking in purpose requires alone time with just you and God. It is the ability to endure seasons of suffering, pain, and even grief that often leads you to a purposeful existence. It is behind the pain that lies God's perfect plan and purpose for our lives. We must take off the mask of strength and perfection to get to the place where God can really use us. I am not saying being strong is a bad thing. However, if we are not careful, that strength can become a mask or may even form a wall that hinders us from receiving the breakthrough that we need to become in sync with our inner Goddess, our divine feminine, which gives us the ability to create balance in the world and fruitfulness.

If you dare to allow God to lead you to purpose, then you will discover a version of yourself that will blow your mind! She is a better you, healed, whole, and unafraid of walking into the power and authority of what God says about you. In my experience, I have learned that it is not about the doors that open and lead you to walking in purpose, but it is often the doors that close that humbles us to a place where we must fully submit ourselves to God's divine will for our lives. The thing about purpose is that it is being formed in the most uncomfortable places in life. Just know that God is right there in that valley with you, ushering you through your wounds, your tears, and fears while He is preparing you for greater. That greater place in you which glorifies God. Ask yourself, who must I become to walk in my purpose? *Ephesians 4:11 "So, Christ himself gave the apostles, the prophets, the evangelists, the pastors, and teachers, to equip his people for works of service, so that the body of Christ may be built up.*

Walking in purpose requires humility, empathy for others, kindness, strength, peacefulness, and gentleness, but it also requires us to walk boldly in the knowledge that it is not for us; it is for the building of God's Kingdom. Walking in purpose requires us to lay down ego, pride, perfection, greediness, and self-gratitude so that other people can see the hand of God through us to lead them into the light and knowledge of God.

Beauty Secret

Look in the mirror each day and affirm that you can do All things through Christ, which strengthens you. Make this your daily routine, then take a step toward something that you have been wanting to do, or toward who it is you desire to become.

Journal your thoughts

Chapter 7

Change Your Hair, Start Over

So, I have this thing that I do when I want to start fresh, whether it is from a stressful week, a negative experience, or even when I decide that it is time to change course and walk with a new outlook on my life, which is, change my hair! I know it could seem to be something simple that really does not mean anything, but to me, it is a spiritual act of shedding unwanted negative energies because I believe that hair not only holds on to impurities and dirt from the environment but also negative energy.

Therefore, something as simple as changing your hair or look refreshes your mood, which directly affects your mental state, making you look better, feel better, and accomplish more. Many studies have been performed on how the effects of stress and trauma can show up in your appearance by way of thinning hair, skin disorders, and brittle nails and can also cause hormonal imbalances that greatly affect your health.

If you follow me on my social media, then you know to expect to see me with a new hairstyle every few days, followed by some sort of motivation to inspire a positive change in your thoughts. This trend I have begun did not begin from watching reality TV, celebrities, nor did it begin when I embarked into the beauty industry, but it was embedded in me from childhood. I grew up in a family that puts a big emphasis on appearance and always looking your best. My mother, as well as my aunts, all had some level of hairstyling abilities, and I watched my mother dress up and do her hair often. Being the youngest child of three, I observed everything around me, including how important it was for my mother to keep herself and her children clean and well-dressed, especially living in subsidized housing. This was to show us that although we were not rich, we still were just as good as those who were, no matter the struggle. My mother would style my hair in assorted styles on a daily using the cutest hair bows and sometimes beads, which she invested in often, especially surrounding school time, and she kept them in a big bucket that she often cleaned out to make sure it stayed organized and tangle-free. Each day, I could expect a cute new hairstyle and a beautiful outfit, which gave me, as a child, the most confidence in myself. My mother also modeled this in front of my sister and me as she would even dress up and change her hair when she went to conduct her business. Then, I saw my mother experience severe depression, and some days, she did not care about her appearance at all.

On these days, Mom seemed incredibly sad, and sometimes angry, these were dark days, not like the days when she pranced in front of the mirror, dressed up, and watched her reflection as she talked on the phone or sang and danced to her favorite music selections. During that time, however, I noticed that she seemed to feel other than her normal self because, in those moments, she did not express her usual vibrant beauty. At least, that's how I saw her. It was during these times that she would allow me to practice styling her hair or doing her makeup, and when I did a decent job, she would instantly perk up or, as she would say, get a pep in her step, lol. Now, as a licensed cosmetologist, hair restoration specialist, and person who cares for people, I have witnessed clients a lot like how my mother was during her dark moments.

When they arrive for their hair appointment, some of my clients are not just there for hair maintenance but because they have experienced some life-altering experiences and need a transformation.

After choosing a style to enhance their outer appearance and which complements their lifestyle, I have been anointed to also pour into them spiritually, not just making them look their best outwardly but reminding them of their inner strength and beauty. This is when I notice an instant shift in their self-confidence! I get to witness how energized and joyful they seem, as well as how confident they become in their readiness to embrace their next!

Changing your hair can mean anything you need it to mean for your journey, and it could be a change in your daily habits or a taking a new course, but whatever the change is for you, take it as a sign of starting anew, shaking off the old habits, and choosing to find new hope in your ability to show up as your best self for ALL that God has in store for your life!

When choosing a new hairstyle, however, the key is to find a style that enhances your natural beauty. Whether using extensions or your natural hair, remember it is about if you are feeling your best and looking your best and not looking like anyone else. I see people choose styles that look great on someone else or on a picture but remember that God has made you unique with unique features, different facial structures, hair types, and textures; therefore, what looks great on someone else may not compliment your beauty the same. It is like the moment in the Bible, 1 Samuel 17 when David realized that he could not fit into Saul's armor and decided to show up in his own way in what fit him. The goal is to feel great about yourself. Choosing the wrong hairstyle can do the complete opposite.

Choose a stylist who can achieve a custom look that best suits you; it will help you to see Yourself better and ultimately feel better. We are all different. Psalms 139:14 says, *"I praise you because I am fearfully and wonderfully made, your works are wonderful, I know that full well.* When David spoke this Psalm to God, it was the revelation that God knows him entirely as He formed him even before conception. This is what we must embrace about ourselves that we are all different from another, and therefore, We must first seek to know the creator that knows us so that we may understand our own divine uniqueness. You are amazing, you are bold as a lion, you are you, and we must change anything that is around and within us that no longer serves where we are going in life or who we must become, as well as what we must do when we arrive. Let us start by changing our hair, but let no one other than you and the Lord change you!

Beauty secrets:

-Take a multi-vitamin every day to support healthy hair, skin, and nails (Consult with your doctor first)
-drink plenty of water
-listen to some form of motivation and spiritual guidance (I love Sarah Jakes Roberts)
-Change your hair

Journal your thoughts

Chapter 8

Embrace Your Flaws

WE ALL HAVE FLAWS! That is a fact: if you are a believer and you have studied any of Jesus's chosen people, they all had some issue or imperfection, whether in statute or character, and were not disqualified from receiving the anointing of the Lord. When I say embrace your flaws, what it really means is to accept that we all have imperfections, faults, and weaknesses that can make us feel unqualified and unprepared for the calling on our lives. However, God specifically tells us in 2 Corinthians 12:9, *"My grace is sufficient for you, for my power is made perfect in weakness."* In the book of 2 Corinthians, Paul has a profound revelation from God, to delights in his weakness so that Gods power may rest on him. Paul has vision and revelations from God that calls for him to realize that it is better to boasts in his weaknesses so that he does not become conceited but remain in a posture of humility. He says, "That is why, for *Christ's sake*, I delight in weaknesses, in insults, in hardships, in persecutions, in difficulties. For when I am weak. Then I am strong." Each of our flaws are our own thorn in the flesh that gives us purpose and reason to cry out to God and gain His Holy power in our lives. This power offers us renewed strength amid any tragedy or forms of opposition that revolts against us in our lives. God uses our unique flaws to shift our perspective in the face of the hardships we experience in our lives. When we surrender, he then develops our spirit man so that he may be glorified, and as a result, we will attract and reach more people who will seek him and come into the full knowledge of who he is within them. This is his will to further expand the kingdom of heaven on earth. One known device of the enemy is to make you believe that what God said to you and about you is not true, which leads to further doubts and insecurities that cause you to feel condemned rather than convicted. Your gifts and talents were given to you by God and when you discover them, it is up to you to use them for God's purpose. God is already aware of your weaknesses and what we must do is submit those things to Him in prayer so that we are able to walk in full victory and dominion in the areas you have been given grace.

For years. I have tried to strive for perfection, not realizing that it was through my imperfections that the Lord wanted to use me. Through my past mistakes and my physical flaws, the Holy Spirit affirmed that I was more than enough, more than enough to reach his people, more than enough to reach some woman, man, or child who is struggling in chains of bondage, and more than enough to fully leave my footprint on this earth. I submit to you that when you surrender your flaws to God and pray, "Lord, what do you want me to do with this: teen pregnancy, addiction, depression, fear, or whatever that weakness is," he will heal and restore your soul. Although those things exist it does not mean that they are who you are. Offer every unclean and painful thing up to God and allow the

Holy Spirit to guide you as you walk into a complete renewal and peacefulness from within. Remember, God makes no mistakes, and you are still worthy!

Think about something

Journal your thoughts

Think about something about yourself, or your life, that you consider a flaw. Take a moment to reflect on how it has helped you grow, learn, or develop resilience in your life.

Chapter 9

Glow Get It

Once you have come into your God-given identity fully accepting who you are to become; the opportunity will come for you to step forward in faith to carry out the dreams and goals that God has placed in your heart. You may have seen visions and received revelation about your life mission, so it is important to trust the path God has for seeing those things manifest in this physical realm. There is an appointed time for all things, so we must have faith in God, work, and wait for them to fall into our laps.

Truth is, while you are waiting on God, He is, in fact, waiting on you to make a move. His Word tells us that faith without works is dead, so we must still work towards our goals and be properly positioned to receive the blessings that we are believing God for. This is where you must Glow Get it!

To glow is to be illuminated, to give out steady light without flame, to shine, to bloom, in other words, to give off a light from within. When you decide to pursue greatness in your life that is in alignment with your purpose, there is a certain glow that God gives you that shines light to the world. What creates that light is the confidence that rises within you once you have decided to live a pure and holy life in Christ. Your light will be seen in every area of your life, including your health, career, rooms you enter, and people you meet. This kind of light is one that serves notice to any spirit of darkness that dares to try and block you! It is important to understand that not only should we glow, but that God gave us this light to draw people unto him! Our gifts make room for us to serve Gods people blessing them; so that He is exalted in the earth; not just to shine to be seen by men but so God gets the glory through us. In fact, the Word of the Lord tells us in *Matthew 5:14, "You are the light of the world. A town built on a hill cannot be hidden."* Notice how people are always complimenting you on the things that you find insignificant about yourself or may even be insecure about; those are usually the most appealing attributes that people see in you. Pray and ask God what to do with it. Know that no matter how hard you try to hide and shrink into the background, it will not work because God has already chosen you to be His hands and even mouthpiece here on earth. We have been commanded to not only pursue the kingdom of heaven from here on earth but to be the light that shines in whatever we do well. *In Matthew 5:15-16; the Lord tells us that "Neither do people light a lamp and put it under a bowl. Instead, they put it on its stand, and it gives light to everyone in the house. In that same way, let your light shine before others, that they may see your good deeds and glorify your Father in heaven."* The key takeaway of the text is that, just like a lamp on its stand, we, too, are ordained to be the light of the world and not hide our light from others.

There is an important purpose for each of us, and we have an opportunity to show up in our families, various industries, and this world. Therefore, hiding will only prevent someone who needs your light from getting the breakthrough that they have been praying for. God made us to be an answer! Your light has a place in the open where people can see how God is working through you and can inspire them to pursue their own dreams and goals and, moreover, inspire them to stop hiding and let their own lights shine to the world.

Now, I believe in making time for self-care and development. Yes, I promote it, but that process may not take as long if we allow the Holy Spirit to heal and transform us within. Inner healing leads us to wholeness, which brings inner peace. Self-care can be activities that nurture that inner tranquility that comes when we truly trust in God's plan for our lives. It helps us to rest and recharge so that we are ready for purpose. God gives us vision, but he cannot make us move on it. That task is the assignment that the Lord has given us rulership over, so let us glow up and get our blessings! Sometimes, the enemy will try to block us from pursuing the things of God but sowing fear and doubt into our minds, and there are also times when we can be our own worst enemy by delaying or even blocking ourselves from the promises that has be already given to us, by God. A few are negative self-talk, a lack of self-control, not seeking wise counsel before making serious decisions about our lives; as well as by being fearful, or disobedient, or simply lacking faith in your own abilities.

Let us take a moment to reflect on the things that we could be doing that are delaying or blocking you from being a Glow-Getter for the kingdom. Negative self-talk is at the top of the list; how many of us have had a dream or vision that we believe came from God, but then, because of our self-doubt, we begin speaking negatively about it? "I do not have enough money to begin, I do not have the support of my loved ones or friends, I need this or that so that I can begin; are all part of a lack mentality. God tells us in his word, Matthew 6:33, "But seek first his kingdom and his righteousness, and all these things will be given to you as well. There is no need to worry about what is missing in the natural because its already in God's plan to give us all that we need for whatever we need it for, and if God called you to it, then you have everything that you need to take hold of it.

Having a lack of self-discipline is another reason that you could delay your progress to the promise. Not having restraint in how we use our resources can delay us from seeing the promise. Also not using wisdom when selecting the company we keep or the places we go because it is written that, "bad company, corrupts good character," and it is important have discernment about who you allow near you when you are in a season of planting and harvest. Managing the aptitudes of your mental, emotional, and spiritual self is also the key to not delaying purpose in your life. Having balance is important so that you are sensitive to receive divine direction. God will give us an idea that will shift an entire generation and change the trajectory if your life for the better but to discern the voice of this divine compass, we must be clear within our spirit. To experience an evolution in life that will expand us and get us to the purpose designed for our life, self-discipline is advised so that we can properly prepare ourselves.

Seek wise counsel, find a mentor, someone who is knowledgeable about the task ahead of you, do your research, and pray to ask God to send you the right people to help guide you through your process of manifesting the vision set before you, do not lean to your own understanding. *1 King 22:5 tells us, "First seek the counsel of the Lord,"* while *Proverb 12:15 reveals that; "The way of fools seems right to them, but the wise listen to advice."* If the vision God gave you only requires your knowledge and hand, then it is too small, and we must then question if it was sent by God in the first place. For the things of God require His people, and there is always someone anointed in the area that our Father has instructed. When you trust Him and obey Him, he will send the other people who are connected to His vision because it is never about us, and it is never for us alone. Wait on the Lord, for God told one of his minor prophets in the book of *Habakkuk 2:2-3 to "Write the vision and make it plain on the tablets, so that he may run who reads it.* The vision is yet for an appointed time. Though it tarries, wait for it because it will surely happen." I love the NIV translation that reads, "It will certainly come and will not delay." That vision or revelation that God has spoken over your life is yet to come to pass, but you must believe that it will happen when it is supposed to and will not delay, therefore be careful not to be out of positioning to receive the vision and better yet do not be the cause of any delay because the Lord showed it to you for a reason so your job is to pray on it, pray over it, pray for it and do the work and wait for it to come at its perfect time. Every perfect gift from God has a divine and perfect timing connected to it, so there is no need to rush or be anxious about it. You got this, and God's got you!

Fear is a stronghold that can cripple us as believers from doing the work to receive the glory connected to our lives. *2 Timothy 1:7 states that "For God has not given us a spirit of fear and timidity but of power, love, and self-discipline."* In verse six, the Lord reminds us to fan into flames the spiritual gift God gave us when he created us. When you let fear stop you from shining, then all you are doing is damping down the Gifts that were placed inside of you from God. Have faith even when fear is present because it just means that we are human-like when we fear the unknown, but we must overcome or conquer this fear by choosing to move forward in faith, strengthening our spiritual man so that we are not delaying the visions that the Lord has spoken over you.

Remember what God said to you, often we get a word from the Lord, we question if it was really spoken because our current circumstances do not look like what we envisioned it to look like to be ready to receive that word. We must continue to seek, pray, fast, and wait patiently to hear further instructions amid any confusion or doubt that could arise against us after the Lord has spoken a word. This practice is the ultimate posture of faith at work in our lives because we must first believe in what God said, and then we have to be obedient in moving toward that word. Seeking God daily allows us to discern the voice of the Lord concerning the matter. If you believe that God told you to quit your job and start your own business, first seek Him, and ask the Lord, I hear you, and I will obey; now, please show me how to move on this word. If God said it, He would show how to accomplish it. How will you know it was the Lord?

Psalms 29:4 says, "The voice of the Lord is powerful; the voice of the Lord is majestic." Psalms 29:11 continues with, "The Lord renews the strength of his people that waits on him, and the Lord blesses them with peace." When God speaks, it is powerful, almost nagging to the spirit; it will cause you to an awareness that will almost come with this inner knowing and strength to move forward, and you will have peace in that word. If you do not experience these things, then maybe you need to continue to seek the Lord until you receive clarity. Nonetheless, do not delay what God wants to do through you; know that you are the right person for the job; just have faith and Glow Get It!

Journal your thoughts

Honor The Beauty That Is Deep Inside of You

You are beautiful, you are loved, you are strong, you are powerful, you are smart, you are gifted, you have purpose, you are more than a conqueror, and you are worthy. You were made in the image of God; therefore, he knows you because he formed you in your mother's womb. He knows you down to the number of hairs on your head. In every trial you faced, God was there. When the trauma occurred, God saw, and he felt the pain you felt. When the relationship ended, God already knew the emptiness it left and began to fill you again. When you failed at that thing, God already had a bigger plan in motion." 1 Peter 3:3-4 the Lord reminds us that our beauty comes from within and is of great worth in God's sight. Therefore, first, give honor to the creator because he has never left you, and he knew that you would go through what you have and that you would be where you are, and yet He still chose you! Remember that all things work together for the good of those who love Him and are called according to his purpose, so honor the fact that you earned every stripe and that if you went through it and came through unharmed, then that is power inside of you that you have yet to tap into.

Honor that inner beauty that is gentle, yet strong, and resilient, trusting in the Lord and allowing Him to order your steps. Honor the

the fact that you did not give up on your dreams when the rejection came when fear tried to cripple you, you kept pursuing what you loved. Honor the love for yourself that gave you the strength to keep pressing when they hurt you. You stayed beautiful, you dared to believe that there was better waiting for you. Honor your courage and the determination it took for you to sit with yourself and seek healing instead of approval; that season where you felt hidden was God planting you and stabilizing your roots so that you would grow into your true, authentic, beautiful self. God's presence is the most beautiful thing about each one of us; the will of God is that we desire more of God's presence, and his beauty and splendor will highlight the beauty that lies deep within us. That smile is given by the joy of the Lord that glow that you have because God restored your peace, and that confidence that you have because the Lord has been your keeper are the essence of what beauty really is.

Nobody ever said life would be easy. We were created to solve a problem on the earth, so consider every one of your obstacles training or, better yet, opportunities for development and growth. Know that every one of your unique qualities will be used to draw the people connected to your answer! It is time to appreciate all of who you are and dig deep to unleash all that God has put inside of you. Some other ways to honor yourself could be to devote some time each day to filling your own bucket, simply acknowledge what strides you've made that day, whether it's that you have completed your to do list or maybe you made time to simply take a walk and exhale for a moment. Just make sure you spend time admiring and loving on yourself for a chance. It will make a difference in how you show up in the world, and most importantly, it will make a difference in who you show up as, the way God has created you to show up. Just as you are, authentic and free.

Honor your mind! Mental health is a real issue in our communities today, so we must guard our minds against worry, stress, and negative thoughts. Use discernment when interacting with people, and do not allow anyone to speak negatively over you. The Word tells us in Philippians 4:8 to focus on what is noble, right, pure, lovely, and admirable, so take time to release all any negative thoughts, either through meditation or even breathing exercises, that allows that release to happen.

Honor your bodies! Each of us were made in Gods image, no matter our size, shape, or color. When you see yourself, understand that you were created just as God wanted you. Therefore, we must honor our body through leading a healthy lifestyle of regular exercise, eating habits, and healing practices. We have an important assignment that will need our full energy and mobility to accomplish so be good to your vessel; you only get one.

We are all a divine expression of God's ultimate idea of beauty. When you were created, the Lord said it was good, so know that nothing that was created by God is bad. Beauty comes from the inside, and it shines outwardly. Look beautiful, dress beautifully, create beautiful, but most importantly, express beautifully through your behavior. What good is a beautiful exterior if the soul is ugly and mean? Although disappointments may occur and trouble may come, know that the beautiful thing is that we get to wake up each day and breathe the air of life! Honor your beautiful life and do amazing things with it!

Woman of God, I pray that this book has opened your eyes to how beautiful you are and how unique your beauty really is. I pray that you will no longer look for the validation of others to affirm you but rather rest in the identity you have in Christ Jesus, that you are fearfully and wonderfully made, that you are the head and not the tail, and it is okay to now walk in obedience of the calling that is on your life! Continue to grow and develop because what you look like now is not the complete version of who you will be; peace and blessings, Queen.

Journal your thoughts

About the Author

Stephanie is a devoted mother, loving wife, and God-fearing woman whose unwavering faith and commitment to her family form the foundation of her life. With a deep and abiding relationship with God, she finds strength in her spirituality, allowing her to navigate life's challenges with grace, resilience, and purpose. Stephanie holds a Bachelor of Business Administration Degree and is a licensed cosmetologist specializing in hair restoration. As a seasoned salon owner, she has built a thriving business based on her passion for beauty and her dedication to helping others feel confident and empowered. In addition to her salon, Stephanie has extensive experience working in sales, where her business acumen has been key to her success in growing and expanding her ventures. She also serves as a platform artist for Phaze III Beauty Association (Ph3B), where she showcases her skills and shares her knowledge with others in the industry. A true testament to overcoming adversity, Stephanie's journey has been one of perseverance, determination, and unwavering self-belief. She embraces each day with a spirit of empowerment, refusing to let life's hurdles define her. Her beauty stems not only from her outward appearance but from her inner strength—the kind that comes from facing life's toughest moments and emerging victorious. When she's not managing her business or sharing her expertise with others, Stephanie enjoys nurturing her passions. Worship and her deep relationship with God are central to her life, providing her with peace and purpose. She finds joy in gardening, traveling, and exploring the world, while her greatest joy remains being a mother—an honor and privilege that shapes her every decision. Stephanie firmly believes that her relationship with God is the source of her peace and power. It is through her faith that she finds the clarity to prioritize what truly matters, focusing on nurturing her family, growing personally, and impacting those around her. Her wisdom and grace shine through in everything she does, inspiring others to rise above their circumstances and live boldly and authentically. With a heart full of purpose and a life grounded in faith, Stephanie continues to lead by example, showing that true beauty lies not in perfection but in the resilience of the human spirit and the love that binds us all.

www.ingramcontent.com/pod-product-compliance
Lightning Source LLC
Chambersburg PA
CBHW040846120626
46547CB00001B/48